T0107695

Masters of camouflage, no two giraffes share the same spot pattern on their coats.

Giraffe

Giraffes roam across the wide savannahs of Africa. These majestic creatures are taller than any others they come across. A giraffe's height gives it many powers that other animals do not have.

A huge advantage of being tall is access to food. Giraffes can feed on buds and leaves way up high in the treetops, which very few other animals can reach. This can be especially helpful during times of drought, as the plants closest to the ground may have been picked over by other animals. Giraffes love chowing down on the leaves of the acacia tree. They are also able to use their super-long tongues to grab tasty bits from high branches. Week in and week out, giraffes have to roam for kilometers to find all the food they need. After all, they need to eat up to 34 kg (75 lb.) of leaves each day to survive.

Another great advantage of giraffes being so tall is that they are able to look out over their surroundings. This superpower allows giraffes to spy predators from a distance. See a lion making its way closer? Giraffes can run away after seeing an enemy through the treetops.

Mama giraffes also use their height superpower in a different way. They give birth to their babies while standing up! The young may not find this to be so pleasant. After all, they can fall over 1.5 m (5 ft.) to the ground as they are being born. Finally, giraffes are also able to rest while standing up.

Fact File

SCIENTIFIC NAME *Giraffa camelopardalis* (giraffe) CLASS Mammalia (mammal) HEIGHT 4.3–5.8 m (14–19 ft.) WEIGHT 794–1,270 kg (1,750–2,800 lb.) HABITAT Grassland LOCATION Giraffes live in dry savannah areas (wherever trees are found) south of the Sahara Desert. NUTRITION Giraffes are herbivores (plant-eaters). Their favorite food is the leaves of acacia trees. Young giraffes nurse for six to nine months, but start eating leaves around four months old. SOCIAL BEHAVIOR Giraffes tend to roam the grasslands in small groups of about six individuals. Occasionally male giraffes will fight each other by butting heads or their necks. But these battles do not tend to be dangerous. Eventually one giraffe will just give up and walk away. FAMILY + OFFSPRING The gestation period of the giraffe is between 400 and 460 days. Female giraffes usually give birth to one calf at a time. Giraffe mothers and calves form "nursery" groups. One mother will stay to babysit the calves while the other moms go out to socialize or eat. The calves play together in the nursery group. AGE EXPECTATION (LIFE SPAN) 25 years FUN FACT A giraffe's tongue is about 53 cm (21 in.) long! PHYSICAL DESCRIPTION Giraffes are the tallest mammals on earth. They have very long necks. A giraffe's legs are about 183 cm (6 ft.) long—taller than many people! These beautiful animals have spotted coats. And no two giraffes have the same pattern of spots. Their coats act as camouflage, blending in well with the leaves and shadows of the grasslands. CONSERVATION The population of giraffes is decreasing. One reason for this is that livestock is overgrazing in areas where giraffes live. The other is habitat loss. In some parts of Africa there is also a problem with poaching, where giraffes are killed for meat, tail hair, their hides, and so on. Some places, such as Kenya, have started conservation programs to protect giraffes.

King Lion was hosting a big party and all the animals had to attend. Lion wanted to give every animal a gift to prove how good a king he was. Kudu got horns. Donkey and Rabbit got long ears. Giraffe cried, "What about me?" King Lion took away Giraffe's voice for being rude. But Giraffe looked so sad that Lion gave him a special suit and horns. Lion also gave him a long neck to see his enemies from far away. And long legs to be able to run away quickly. Giraffe was thrilled. He trotted away satisfied.

Prized for their perfume-worthy scent, African civets love super-strong smells.

African Civet

On the forest floor in the Congo, an African civet is wandering about. This furry creature is in search of things that have strong scents. As the civet sniffs around, it comes upon a large piece of rotting fruit. While other animals might be repulsed, the African civet finds the scent exciting. What does the civet do? It rubs its body all over the fruit, trying to scent mark it. The civet does the same thing when it runs into a creature called a pangolin. The pangolin is afraid of the civet and lets off a stink that it hopes will scare the civet off. But no luck! The civet rubs its own scent all over the pangolin as well. African civets have a superpower—they make a scented secretion called civetone. This chemical substance can be found in the civet's scent glands, located near the animal's rear end. While African civets use this substance to mark their territories and communicate with other animals, some people use the scent, too—to make perfume!

Historically, people collected civetone as an important ingredient used in perfume. To gather the civetone, African civets were kept in cages. Every few days people would scrape out the animals' scent glands with a special spoon. The animals were not killed for their civetone but they were not allowed to wander freely anymore either. Today, scientists can make a synthetic version of civetone in laboratories. This allows the perfume industry to continue using a similar scent while letting the civets be free.

Fact File

SCIENTIFIC NAME *Civettictis civetta* (African civet) CLASS Mammalia (mammals) LENGTH 61–91 cm (24–36 in.) for body length, 43–61 cm (17–24 in.) for tail WEIGHT 9.5–20 kg (21–44 lb.) HABITAT Secondary forest, woodland, bush areas, and aquatic habitats LOCATION African civets live in many parts of Africa, from Mauritania and Senegal to Ethiopia and southern Somalia, then southwards as far as northeastern South Africa. NUTRITION African civets are omnivores. They eat meat (such as small mammals) as well as fruits, and even crabs or snails in some areas. Young civets nurse on their mother's milk exclusively for about six weeks and then start eating solid food. SOCIAL BEHAVIOR These animals tend to be solitary except during the breeding season when two or more civets may be seen together. They are also territorial and mark their territories by releasing musk from a gland near their rear end. African civets are nocturnal (active at night). FAMILY + OFFSPRING The gestation period for African civets is about 65 days. Females can have two or three litters per year. They usually give birth to between one and four offspring in a litter. Mother civets with young often have nests in holes that other animals have made. AGE EXPECTATION (LIFE SPAN) 15–20 years FUN FACT African civets scream, growl, and make a cough-spitting sound. CONSERVATION In some parts of Africa (such as Gabon and Nigeria), these animals are sold for their meat and skin. Male civets are regularly taken from the wild for their musk production. This can reduce local civet populations, but overall, there are not any major threats to this species at this time.

Uses of the Civet

In southwestern Cameroon, a number of parts of the African civet are used for many different purposes. The nails of this cat are mixed with billy goat weed and are used in rituals to deliver people from evil. African civet skin is used to make drums. Chiefs and elders of the Ekpe society also use the skin for carpet.

Active at night, these omnivorous primates have special features to help them find food in the dark.

Lesser Bushbaby

On a moonless night in the African rainforest, the sky is nearly pitch black. The sounds of many nocturnal creatures pierce the darkness. Up in the canopy, a lesser bushbaby is ready to get moving. One might wonder how this small primate can see anything, let alone move about the forest. However, the bushbaby has a special power—excellent night vision.

This animal's eyes are huge compared to the size of its head. Thanks to its big eyes, the lesser bushbaby can hunt insects, lizards, or even nesting birds—regardless of how dark its habitat is. Many sources say they can see in what people would call total darkness. That is a handy advantage for this tiny hunter!

SCIENTIFIC NAME *Galago senegalensis* (Senegal galago, lesser bushbaby) CLASS Mammalia (mammals) LENGTH 17 cm (7 in.) without tail WEIGHT 95–300 g (3–11 oz.) HABITAT Forest and bush areas LOCATION Africa, south of the Sahara (as far south as Tanzania and Kenya); also some nearby islands, including Zanzibar NUTRITION Lesser bushbabies are omnivores. They love to eat grasshoppers but also eggs, small birds, seeds, fruits, and flowers. Young bushbabies usually nurse for around three and a half months. SOCIAL BEHAVIOR Lesser bushbabies are social creatures. They tend to sleep in groups made of several individuals, though they carry out their evening activities alone. These animals are nocturnal (active at night). FAMILY + OFFSPRING The gestation period of lesser bushbabies is 110 to 120 days. These bushbabies breed twice each year. Females usually have one or two offspring per litter. They give birth and raise their young in a nest of leaves. AGE EXPECTATION (LIFE SPAN) 3–4 years (in the wild), 10 years (in captivity) FUN FACT Lesser bushbabies can jump 3–5 m (10–16 ft.) in a single leap!

Aye-Aye

It is nighttime in the rainforest of Madagascar. An aye-aye stretches out after being curled up all day in its nest of branches and leaves. When looking for food in the treetops, the aye-aye has a special feature. Its middle finger is long and narrow, almost like that of a skeleton. Sometimes the aye-aye uses this special finger to tap on trees. Why? So that it can listen to see if any insect larvae are moving underneath the tree's bark. The aye-aye also uses its middle finger to dig out the insects from the tree. And sometimes an aye-aye scoops out the flesh of mangoes or coconuts it wants to eat!

SCIENTIFIC NAME *Daubentonia madagascariensis* (aye-aye) CLASS Mammalia (mammals) LENGTH 35.6–43.2 cm (14–17 in.) for head and body, 55.9–61 cm (22–24 in.) for tail WEIGHT 1.8 kg (4 lb.), 90–140 g (3–5 oz.) at birth HABITAT Rain forest, deciduous forest, dry scrub forest, and mangrove swamps LOCATION Aye-ayes are only found on the island of Madagascar. NUTRITION Aye-ayes are omnivores. They eat nuts, nectar, insect larvae, fungi, and fruits. These creatures are known for raiding coconut plantations. In the wild, young aye-ayes are weaned as early as seven months old. SOCIAL BEHAVIOR Aye-ayes are largely solitary creatures. Adults spend most of their lives on their own, except for during courtship (breeding) times. Aye-ayes are nocturnal (active at night). FAMILY + OFFSPRING The gestation period for aye-ayes is about 170 days. Females usually give birth one offspring at a time. There is normally a two to three year interval between births. AGE EXPECTATION (LIFE SPAN) 20 years in the wild FUN FACT Some tribes in northern Madagascar think that the aye-aye is a sign of evil to come. CONSERVATION Aye-ayes are endangered species. The main threats to their survival are habitat loss and hunting. Sometimes farmers hunt aye-ayes because they are a threat to their crops. In some areas, aye-ayes are also killed because people consider them symbols of bad luck or evil.

Equipped with scales, pangolins can roll up into a ball and avoid even their fiercest predators.

Pangolin

It is nighttime in the African savannah. A hungry ground pangolin has come out of its den. With its hard brown scales, it looks like an anteater ready for battle. Despite its poor eyesight, the scaly creature finds a termite mound using its strong sense of smell. It uses its sharp claws to tear apart the mound. It flicks its tongue, rapid fire. It is a termite feast!

While the pangolin is chowing down, another predator is on the prowl. It is a lion. Despite the darkness, the lion has caught a glimpse of the pangolin. The lion crouches in the tall grass, stalking silently. He has his eyes set on the scaly termite cruncher.

Just before the lion can make a meal of the pangolin, the pangolin seems to make itself disappear. It rolls up into a tight, almost-perfect ball, with its face and underside tucked deep within. The lion swats at the ball, which rolls across the grassy ground. The lion tries to bite through the ball. But the hard scales are too tough. These scales are made of keratin, the same material as your fingernails. The edges of the scales are sharp enough to hurt the attacker. After a few minutes of batting and biting, the lion gives up. The pangolin's superpower has saved its life.

Fact File

SCIENTIFIC NAME *Manis temminckii* (ground pangolin) CLASS Mammalia (mammal) LENGTH 40–70 cm (16–28 in.) for head and body and about the same for its tail WEIGHT 7–18 kg (15–40 lb.). At birth, a pangolin weighs 200–500 g (7–18 oz.). HABITAT Pangolins prefer to live in areas with sandy soils. They can be found in forests, savannahs, open grasslands, and places with thick brush. Pangolins can thrive both in areas with high or low rainfall. LOCATION Ground pangolins are found in central, eastern, and southern Africa. Their range stretches from Sudan and Chad, down through Tanzania and Kenya, all the way south to the northern sections of South Africa. NUTRITION The diet of a ground pangolin is mostly made up of ants and termites, though they sometimes eat soft-bodied insects or larvae. It is estimated that a pangolin can eat up to around 70 million insects per year. Baby pangolins start eating termites at around one month old. Since they do not have teeth, pangolins swallow sand and small stones to help grind up their food. This helps their stomachs break down food for digestion. SOCIAL BEHAVIOR Pangolins are very shy. They tend to be solitary creatures except briefly during mating season. Pangolins are also nocturnal. During the day, they often rest in burrows they make in the ground. FAMILY + OFFSPRING Females give birth to single offspring in underground dens. When pangolins are born, their scales are soft and pale. These start to harden by their second day of life. The young stay in their dens for about a month. Females are typically alone with their offspring. When infant pangolins first leave the den with their mothers, they often ride on the base of her tail. AGE EXPECTATION (LIFE SPAN) 20 years FUN FACT A pangolin's tongue can be more than 40 cm (16 in.) long when fully extended! PHYSICAL DESCRIPTION Pangolins are covered in scales yet they are not reptiles. They have been described as "walking artichokes"! The animals have small heads and broad, long tails. They have no teeth. But their tongues are very sticky—great for catching ants and termites! Pangolins have a strange way of walking. Their front legs are shorter than their back legs and have huge claws. So they shuffle along, tucking their front claws under them as they walk. CONSERVATION The pangolin is one of earth's most threatened species. Some people hunt these animals for their meat, which is considered a delicacy. Others hunt them for their scales, which are used in traditional Chinese medicine and are believed to cure ailments from asthma to cancer.

A Story About How Pangolin Provided A Feast

Pangolin and Leopard became very good friends. Pangolin invited Leopard to visit him at his home. Leopard brought all his wives to Pangolin's village. But Pangolin had nothing to cook. Pangolin went on a hunt and came to a huge tree. He climbed this tree and rolled down in a ball. An okpweng (a type of antelope) saw this feat and asked Pangolin how to do it. Pangolin said to climb the tree and fall down slowly. The okpweng tried it—but fell and died. That's how Pangolin got the meat to feed his guests.

Pangolin

–

Even the king of the jungle is no match for the tightly knitted and sharp-edged scales of the pangolin.

Champions of camouflage, these reptiles love to eat a variety of insects.

Common Flat-tail Gecko

In a Madagascan forest, a leaf-tailed gecko rests all day. Its head faces down. Its legs and spatula-shaped tail are stretched out, almost flattened against the bark of a tree. Most people would walk by this gecko and never see it. In fact, the leaf-tailed gecko has a special frill of skin that helps blend the animal's outline into the tree. This gecko can change its color to blend in better with darker or lighter tree bark. Its powers of camouflage are absolutely incredible!

While the leaf-tailed gecko is a master of disguise, there are times when it can shock with color. If a predator threatens it, this gecko will use a cool but colorful defensive strategy—it opens its mouth wide to show a bright orange-red inside and lets off a loud distress call.

SCIENTIFIC NAME *Uroplatus fimbriatus* (common leaf-tailed gecko, common flat-tail gecko) CLASS Reptilia (reptile) LENGTH Up to 30 cm (12 in.) HABITAT Tropical rainforests LOCATION The common flat-tailed gecko is only found on the island of Madagascar. NUTRITION Leaf-tailed geckos are carnivores. The bulk of their diet is insects, though they will also occasionally eat small rodents or reptiles. SOCIAL BEHAVIOR These geckos are nocturnal (active at night). FAMILY + OFFSPRING Females typically lay one or two eggs at a time. These eggs tend to hatch after 90 to 120 days. FUN FACT These geckos can see in color even at night! CONSERVATION The population of these geckos is decreasing. They are threatened by deforestation, which is the result of fire and clearing land for agriculture.

Carpet Chameleon

It is early morning in eastern Madagascar. A carpet chameleon walks along the branch of a tree until it finds a sunny spot. The chameleon uses its superpower—color changing—to make its body a dark color. This way the chameleon can soak up more of the sun's rays and warm itself more effectively. Why? Carpet chameleons usually begin hunting for prey once they have reached their ideal body temperature.

Once warmed up, the chameleon ventures out in search of prey. Sometimes the chameleon might be a bright green color. Other times it is green with a brown, black, and white speckled pattern. That is why this creature is called a carpet chameleon—some people think its designs look like an Oriental carpet.

Chameleons change their color for many reasons. They use color changes to communicate with other chameleons, sending messages about their moods, or to make themselves more attractive to mates. They also change color in response to the temperature, humidity, or the amount of light in their surroundings.

The chameleon looks in two different directions for something to munch on. Perhaps a cricket, or a grasshopper? The chameleon catches sight of one. Quick as a flash, it sticks out its long, sticky tongue. Splat! The chameleon's tongue is like a suction cup. It grabs the insect and quickly pulls the prey into its mouth where it can crush and swallow its meal.

SCIENTIFIC NAME *Furcifer lateralis* (carpet chameleon, jeweled chameleon, white-lined chameleon) CLASS Reptilia (reptile) LENGTH 17–25 cm (7–10 in.) WEIGHT A newborn carpet chameleon weighs around the same as four toothpicks! HABITAT These chameleons often live on the edges of forests and in shrubby grassland areas. They also thrive in altered or disturbed habitats and even gardens with enough vegetation. LOCATION Carpet chameleons are only found on the island of Madagascar. NUTRITION Carpet chameleons live almost entirely on a diet of insects. They commonly eat flies, crickets, grasshoppers, and insect larvae. SOCIAL BEHAVIOR Males are very territorial and will posture, change color, and even hiss to scare off other male rivals. Carpet chameleons are diurnal (active during the day). They typically spend the early part of the day warming up their bodies and then will hunt for prey during the remainder of the daylight hours. FAMILY + OFFSPRING Females usually lay between eight and 23 eggs at a time. They deposit their eggs in a depression they make in the soil. Females can produce as many as three clutches of eggs in a single year. The eggs need to incubate for about six months at a temperature of around 24°C (75°F). AGE EXPECTATION (LIFE SPAN) Carpet chameleons rarely live longer than three years. FUN FACT Chameleons can rotate and focus each of their eyes separately.

Even when the sun heats the air up to 40°Celsius (104°F), dromedaries are amazing at desert survival and thrive where many animals cannot.

Dromedary

It is a typical summer day in the Sahara Desert—very hot and very dry. This whole region gets less than 10 cm (4 in.) of rain per year. And temperatures can skyrocket to over 57°C (135°F)! One might wonder how any living creature could survive in such a harsh environment. Dromedaries are amazing desert-dwellers. They have many adaptations that allow them to thrive in some of the driest places on earth. Dromedaries can close their nostrils to keep out sand. They have long eyelashes—two rows of them!—to protect their eyes from sand. Their bushy eyebrows help with this task, too.

Have you ever seen a dromedary eating thorny bushes? While this would be painful for humans, it is no problem for a dromedary. They have thick, tough lips that can munch on whatever prickly or rough plants are around. And the dromedary's large, thick footpads help it get around well despite the desert's shifting sands and rocky terrain.

When it comes to saving water, dromedaries are superheroes. This creature's hump stores as much as 36 kg (80 lb.) of fat. This camel can break the fat down into energy—and water—when needed. The hump gives a dromedary its famous ability to travel as much as 161 km (100 mi.) through the desert without a drink. And dromedaries rarely sweat, so they do not lose their precious water this way. But when these animals drink, they are like sponges. A thirsty dromedary can drink 113 L (30 gal.) of water in just 13 minutes!

Fact File

SCIENTIFIC NAME *Camelus dromedarius* (Arabian camel, dromedary) CLASS Mammalia (mammal) HEIGHT Over 2.1 m (6.9 ft.) at the hump LENGTH 2.2–3.4 m (7.2–11.2 ft.) for body, 51 cm (20 in.) for tail WEIGHT Up to 726 kg (1,600 lb.) HABITAT Desert LOCATION Dromedaries live in northern Africa—most famously in the Sahara Desert. They are also found in southwest Asia and were introduced to Australia. NUTRITION Dromedaries are herbivores (plant-eaters). They mostly eat dry grasses, thorny plants, and saltbush. Dromedary calves nurse on their mother's milk for up to one or two years but they start eating grass around two to three months old. SOCIAL BEHAVIOR Dromedaries typically live in groups of 2–15 or 20 animals. They tend to live in family units with one male, one or more (up to several) females, and both young and subadult members. Except during mating season, dromedaries are not aggressive in nature. They usually walk in single file when traveling. Dromedaries are diurnal (active during the day). FAMILY + OFFSPRING The gestation period of dromedaries is about 12–14 months. Females give birth to a single calf. Very rarely they have twins. Most dromedary calves are born at the end of March or April. Calves can stand and walk not long after birth. The newborn calves tend to stay with their mother for about two weeks then return to join their family herd. AGE EXPECTATION (LIFE SPAN) 40–50 years FUN FACT Camels can move both legs on one side of their body at the same time. PHYSICAL DESCRIPTION Dromedaries are usually caramel or sandy brown in color. They have long, curved necks and a narrow but deep chest. These camels are known for the single hump on their back.

The Story of Stork and Camel

Mrs. Stork was the hardest-working bird in Egypt. An excellent gardener, she grew many vegetables in a secluded spot where she thought no one could find them. But Monkey and Donkey went into her garden and ate her vegetables. They would not leave when she found them there. Mrs. Stork asked Camel for help. Despite his dribbly mouth, Camel was clever. He said, "It is as clear as the hump on my back to whom this garden belongs." Camel picked up Monkey and tossed him into the river. And he shoved Donkey out of the garden, too. Mrs. Stork and Camel threw a dinner party together that evening.

With their thick skin and fearless attitude, honey badgers are not as sweet as the honey they love.

Honey Badger

It is just after dusk on a grassland in southern Africa. A honey badger comes out of its underground home. A small snake slithers past. The honey badger wastes no time. Chomp! The snake makes a tasty snack. This snake did not have time to strike or bite the honey badger, but that would not have mattered. Honey badgers have very thick skin. And they seem to be immune to snake venom.

The honey badger continues along. As it wanders, it munches on insects and honey it finds. Suddenly the honey badger hears a noise. It seems to be coming from behind. Perhaps it is a predator. The honey badger does not flee. The animal is known for being fearless. It will take on creatures from cobras to leopards to lions. One might think the honey badger would always lose in fights with these much larger animals. But often they survive the battles.

The honey badger moves quickly. So does its enemy. So the honey badger uses its super-smelly powers! At the base of a honey badger's striped tail is a special gland that stores a very stinky liquid. As its predator, a lion, gets too close for comfort, the honey badger drops a "stink bomb"! This odor does not get sprayed over its enemy like that of a skunk. Nor does it last a long time. But the smell is a powerful message—"Get away from me!"

After its close encounter, the honey badger darts into a hole beneath a tree root. And the lion darts away from the horrible stink.

Fact File

SCIENTIFIC NAME *Mellivora capensis* (honey badger, ratel) CLASS Mammalia (mammals) HEIGHT 23–30 cm (9–12 in.) tall at the shoulder LENGTH 73–96 cm (29–38 in.) for body, 14–23 cm (6–9 in.) for tail WEIGHT 6.2–13.6 kg (14–30 lb.), 20 g (0.7 oz.) at birth HABITAT Honey Badgers mainly live in dry areas but can also be found in grasslands and forests. LOCATION From southern Morocco to the southern tip of Africa. Honey badgers also live in Asia. NUTRITION Honey badgers are omnivores. They eat everything from small mammals to reptiles, insects, and even juicy fruits on occasion. And they love honey! SOCIAL BEHAVIOR For the most part, honey badgers are solitary creatures. Males and females normally only get together to mate. Young honey badgers stay with their mothers until between 14 months and 2 years old. During this time, they learn hunting skills. Honey badgers are nocturnal (active at night). They spend most of the daytime sleeping curled up in a ball. FAMILY + OFFSPRING The gestation period for honey badgers is 7–10 weeks. Females usually give birth to one offspring, but occasionally two. Mother honey badgers dig nursery chambers lined with grass to give birth and raise their young (on their own). AGE EXPECTATION (LIFE SPAN) Unknown in the wild. Up to 26 years in zoos (captivity) FUN FACT This animal's skin is so thick it can withstand porcupine quills, bee stings, or even dog bites! PHYSICAL DESCRIPTION Honey badgers have strong but short legs and a flattened, stocky body. Their front feet have long claws for defense and digging. Their fur is mostly black with a wide grayish-white stripe down the back. CONSERVATION Honey badgers are considered endangered in some areas where they live. This is largely due to people encroaching on their territory. Some beekeepers also kill honey badgers, as they are seen as a threat to their beehives. But since honey badgers cannot jump, some beekeepers just set their beehives up higher off the ground—thus protecting the honey and these animals!

The Story of Honey Badger, Lion, and Kalulu

An unusual friendship developed between Honey Badger and Lion. Lion lived in the tall grass on one side of a valley. Honey Badger lived in an unused anthill on the valley's other side. Lion would call across the valley to offer meat to Honey Badger. And Honey Badger would invite Lion to share his honey. One day Kalulu the Hare moved in between the two friends. When Lion called out to offer meat, Kalulu said no. When Honey Badger offered honey, Kalulu said no. Lion and Honey Badger could not figure out what was happening. Then the friends found Kalulu eating grass in the middle of the valley. Lion was about to eat Kalulu when he pounced into a pile of dust. Kalulu sprinted away and was more careful about where he built his home after that.

Honey Badger

–

A honey badger and a fiercely fanged snake engage in a nasty battle.

Silent stalkers, lions are fantastic hunters capable of surprising their prey as they dash out of the grasslands.

Lion

It is nighttime on Africa's Serengeti Plain. Several members of the lion pride are resting in the tall grass. One of the lionesses lifts her head and takes a deep sniff. The scent of buffalo reaches her nostrils. The buffalos must be drinking from the nearby watering hole.
The lioness has not eaten since yesterday. Like the rest of the pride, she is hungry. She rises to her feet. Three of the other lionesses get up as well. They stalk through the grass, making hardly a sound. As they get closer, they notice a buffalo that is limping. The lionesses stalk closer to the watering hole.
The lionesses are super hunters. Without so much as a growl, they agree on what to do. The four of them spread out, making a formation like a fan. Two head directly for the wounded buffalo, which moves in the direction of the long grass. The buffalo does not know that other lionesses are waiting there. Finally, the hunters decide that the buffalo is close enough. They spring forth, scratching and biting the terrified creature. Four fierce lionesses surround their prey. One pins it down against the ground, biting its throat. The buffalo struggles, but within moments it is dead.
The male lions of the pride waste no time in arriving. They claw and snarl at each other, rip the carcass to shreds, and eat until they are satisfied. Then the lionesses and cubs get their share of the meat. After this successful hunt, the pride goes back to sleep—until their next prey arrives on the scene.

Fact File

SCIENTIFIC NAME *Panthera leo* (African lion) CLASS Mammalia (mammals) HEIGHT 123 cm (48 in.) for males, 107 m (42 in.) for females LENGTH 1.4–2.0 m (4.6–6.6 ft.) for head and body, 66.7–100.3 cm (26–39 in.) for tail WEIGHT 120.2–190.5 kg (265–420 lb.), 1.4 kg (3 lb.) at birth HABITAT Savannahs that have thick brush LOCATION Africa, south of the Sahara Desert NUTRITION Lions are carnivores (meat-eaters). They eat everything from antelope and rodents to baby elephants and crocodiles. Lion cubs nurse for about six months. SOCIAL BEHAVIOR Lions are social animals. They live in groups known as prides. A pride is family unit that can include as many as three males, a dozen females, and their offspring. All of the lionesses in a pride are related. Lions do most of their hunting at night. FAMILY + OFFSPRING The gestation period for lions is almost four months. Females often give birth to two or three cubs in a litter. Mothers keep their cubs hidden for about four to six weeks before they return to the pride. And cubs can nurse from any female in the pride, not just their mothers. Male cubs stay with their mothers for about two years, while female cubs may remain with their mothers for life. AGE EXPECTATION (LIFE SPAN) 15–18 years in the wild, about 20 years in captivity (zoos) FUN FACT The roar of a lion can be heard from 8 km (5 mi.) away! PHYSICAL DESCRIPTION African lions have tawny-colored coats. Only the males have manes. CONSERVATION The population of African lions has decreased rather dramatically in recent decades. These animals need big territories to hunt but habitat loss is a real problem for them.

A Good Turn

One day when Lion was hunting he got a thorn stuck in his foot. He tried to get it out himself but could not. Lion was in pain and desperate. He lay down on a path where he knew people would pass by. A man saw Lion and was afraid. But the man recognized Lion's problem. The man used his knife to remove the thorn from Lion's paw. Lion jumped up and ran into the woods. Later, the man found a freshly killed buck on the path. It was Lion's gift to the man. The man shared the meat with his neighbors.

Though they look like swollen sausages, African electric catfish can shock enemies with tremendous power.

Electric Catfish

The electric catfish's superpower is – you guessed it – electricity. This fish is able to hunt and stun its prey in a unique way. It has an electric organ just below the skin on the main part of its body and under part of the tail as well. This electric organ is made up of a type of muscle tissue and forms a gelatin-like layer under its skin.
The shocks emitted by the electric catfish travel from its head towards its tail. Just how powerful is the shock of an electric catfish? That depends on the size of the fish. The bigger the fish, the stronger its electrical discharge. This predator can discharge a shock that is between 350 and 450 volts. Its first discharge tends to be more powerful than the shocks that follow.
The electric catfish uses its electrical powers for different purposes. One is to defend itself. After all, the electric catfish's shocks are powerful enough to stun other fish that get too close. Another reason these catfish use their electrical powers is to capture prey. But you might be surprised to learn that electric catfish do not have great eyesight. They can also use their electrical discharges like a radar to sense nearby objects. This is especially helpful in murky water or at night when the water is dark.

Fact File

SCIENTIFIC NAME *Malapterurus electricus* (electric catfish, african electric catfish) CLASS Actinopterygii (ray-finned fishes) LENGTH Up to 0.9–1.2 m (3–4 ft.) or more WEIGHT Up to 23 kg (51 lb.) HABITAT Freshwater; Electric catfish live in ponds, lakes, streams, and rivers. LOCATION Electric catfish live in northern, western, and eastern Africa. They are found in the Nile River system, as well as in Lake Tanganyika, Lake Chad, and the Senegal basin (among other places). NUTRITION Electric catfish are piscivores (fish-eaters). They tend to feed on whatever prey is easily available within their habitat. SOCIAL BEHAVIOR Electric catfish are quite territorial. They defend their territories aggressively. They often try to scare off other fish using open-mouth displays. They will also bite enemies. Only during especially heated fights will this fish use its electrical powers. Electric catfish are nocturnal (active at night). They pass most of their days hiding under shelter. They hunt most actively in the 4–5 hours after sunset. FAMILY + OFFSPRING Not much is known about the reproductive biology of the electric catfish. Breeding pairs of these fish tend to nest in holes dug out from the clay banks in water that is 1–3 m (3–10 ft.) deep. It is believed that the female lays her eggs in shallow water. Both parents may guard the eggs until they are big enough for the tadpole-shaped larvae (or fry) to hatch. AGE EXPECTATION (LIFE SPAN) Not known FUN FACT Electric catfish can eat prey half their size. PHYSICAL DESCRIPTION Some people say that electric catfish look like swollen sausages. Their bodies are puffy and soft, with a long cylindrical shape. They are usually grayish-brown on their sides and back, and cream or off-white on their underside. They have small eyes and thick lips. Their snout has a rounded shape. Electric catfish have three pairs of barbels, the fleshy filaments around the mouth. CONSERVATION African electric catfish are widely distributed in Africa. They have become rare in the Lower and Upper Nile. The Aswan High Dam has impacted the habitat of these catfish, as they need fast-flowing water to thrive. Pollution of the Nile in Egypt has threatened these fish. So has overfishing in eastern Africa.

The Electric Catfish in Ancient Times

These animals have fascinated people since ancient Egyptian times. In fact, the ancient Egyptians referred to the creatures as "he who had saved many in the seas." Why? When a fisherman found an electric catfish in his net, the catfish would shock the fisherman through contact with the net or perhaps the wet boating pole. This would cause the fisherman to let go of the net, thus freeing his catch.

Equipped with fierce fangs, these spiders often scare off or spit at enemies and prey.

Spitting Spiders

Skittering across the ground by night, a spitting spider is on the prowl. These spiders are stealthy hunters—creepy and quiet. Even though their vision is poor, spitting spiders have other senses and skills to help them catch prey. They roam around with their front legs raised to help them detect prey using the sensory hairs on their feet. If a moth, fly, or another kind of prey is detected, the spitting spider uses its superpower—special spit! Once the prey is within 5–10 mm (0.2–0.4 in.) of the spider, it shoots out two streams of super sticky silk over its victim. This basically glues the prey to the ground (or whatever it is standing on). These spiders can shoot the silk as far as 20 mm (0.8 in.).

This spider's gummy spit is actually a mixture of sticky silk and venom, which paralyzes the spider's prey. The spitting spider can then bite its victim, killing it. Once the prey is dead, the spider will drag it off and suck out its insides. Spit—bite—slurp: another successful hunt!

SCIENTIFIC NAME *Scytodidae* (spitting Spiders) CLASS Arachnida (arachnids) LENGTH Up to 10 mm (0.4 in.) HABITAT Spitting spiders live in a variety of habitats, including grasslands and floodplains. They often live under rocks and logs. LOCATION Spitting spiders are found in locations around the world—from North America and Europe to Asia and Africa. NUTRITION Spitting spiders live on a diet of insects. SOCIAL BEHAVIOR Spitting spiders are solitary animals, interacting only for mating. They are nocturnal (active at night). FAMILY + OFFSPRING After laying their eggs, females use a few strands of silk to hold them together. The females carry the eggs around near their fangs. The eggs hatch about two weeks later. The newly hatched spiders stay with their mothers until the time of their first molts. AGE EXPECTATION (LIFE SPAN) 2–4 years FUN FACT Spitting spiders have poor vision.

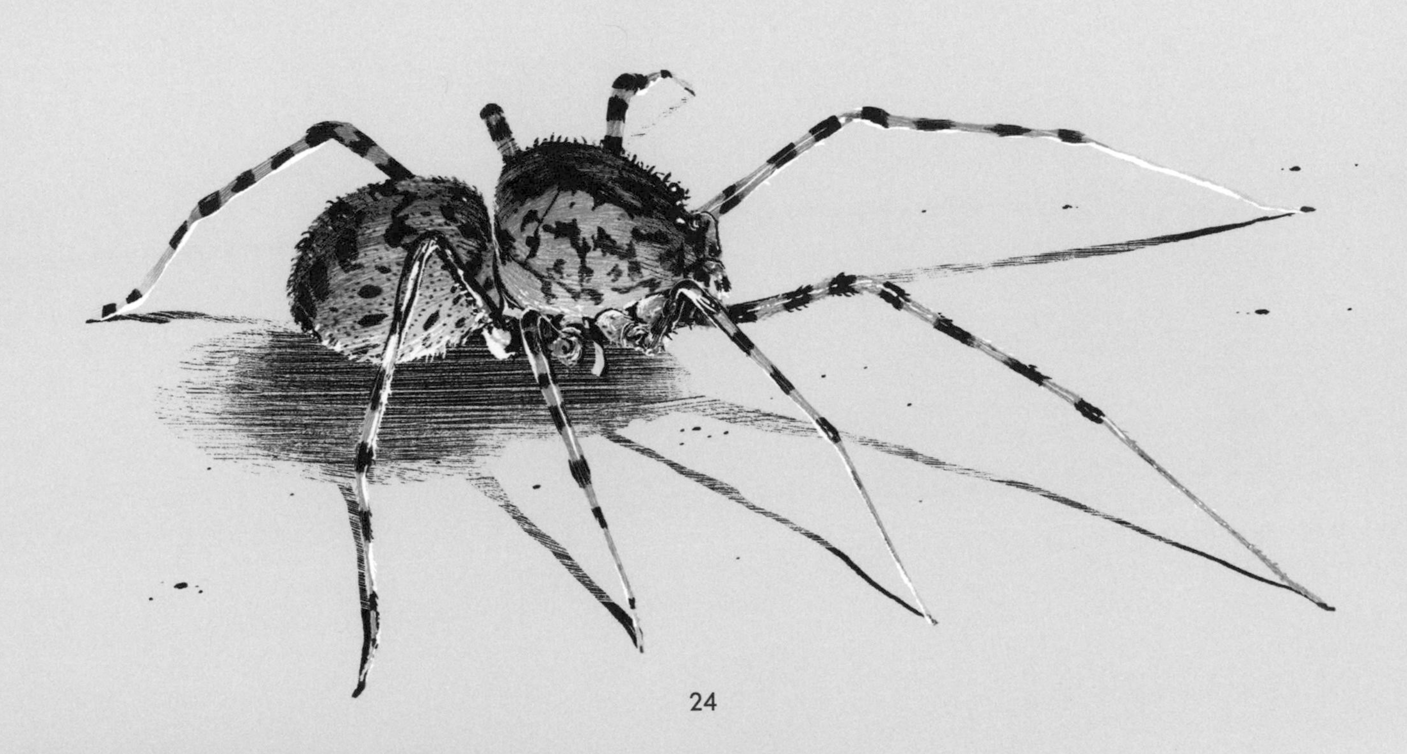

King
Baboon Spider

King baboon spiders are surprisingly popular pets. But you would not want to be the person collecting these scary spiders. Why not? They have a rather nasty temperament and are quite defensive towards people (and other primates). If a king baboon spider is approached, it will rear up and show off its fierce, long fangs. If that is not scary enough for most people, the spider will also rub its legs together to make a loud hissing noise. Look out!

SCIENTIFIC NAME *Pelinobius muticus* (king baboon spider) CLASS Arachnida (arachnids) LENGTH 14–20 cm (6–8 in.) HABITAT Dry scrubland and grasslands LOCATION East Africa—Kenya, Tanzania, and Uganda NUTRITION These spiders are carnivores (meat-eaters). They eat larvae, insects, and small mammals. SOCIAL BEHAVIOR King Baboon spiders often stay inside their burrows, only coming out to find food and water. They are aggressive in nature. These spiders are nocturnal (active at night). FAMILY + OFFSPRING About a month to eight weeks after mating, a female king baboon spider will produce an egg sac. The eggs will incubate and then hatch approximately five to eight weeks later. FUN FACT The fangs of king baboon spiders can be more than 6 mm (0.2 in.) long!

Spectacular shadow boxers, banded mongoose are amazing snake killers.

Banded Mongoose

In the brush lands of southern Africa live many dangerous creatures. Wandering in its daily search for food, a banded mongoose exits the bush and arrives at a clearing. On the other side of the dusty trail sits a black mamba. A single drop of the mamba's venom is enough to kill an adult human. Black mambas are also fast and aggressive. But the banded mongoose is a fierce predator. It, too, moves at lightning speed.

At first glance, it almost looks like the mongoose is shadow boxing. It jumps around, darting to and fro. There is a strategy to the mongoose's movements. The mongoose basically dances in circles around the toxic snake. The mamba repeatedly tries to lash out at the mongoose, which carefully avoids its strikes. The mongoose continues to circle around the snake until the snake is exhausted.

With very careful movements, the banded mongoose makes its killer move. The mongoose gives a quick but effective snap to the back of the mamba's head. This action severs the spine of the snake. The snake is alive but cannot move any longer. With its razor-sharp teeth, the mongoose drags off its 2 m-long (6.6 ft.) prey. The mamba is quite a feast for the banded mongoose. The mongoose will eat well today, thanks to its snake-killing superpower!

Fact File

SCIENTIFIC NAME *Mungos mungo* (banded mongoose) CLASS Mammalia (mammals) HEIGHT 20 cm (8 in.) at the shoulder LENGTH 30–45 cm (12–18 in.), with a 15–30 cm (6–12 in.) tail WEIGHT 1.5–2.5 kg (3–6 lb.). 20 g (0.7 oz.) at birth HABITAT Grasslands, brush lands, woodlands, and rocky areas LOCATION Banded mongooses live south of the Sahara Desert. NUTRITION Banded mongooses mainly eat insects, but they also eat many other foods, such as earthworms, rodents, snakes, and fallen fruit. SOCIAL BEHAVIOR Unlike some mongoose species, banded mongooses are social animals. They live in groups called packs. A pack usually is made up of 10–20 individuals, but sometimes has up to 40 members. Each pack has one dominant male. Banded mongooses are diurnal (active during the day). FAMILY + OFFSPRING The gestation period for banded mongooses is 60 days. Females often give birth to two to six young in a litter. Mothers keep their offspring in their dens for about four weeks before taking them out for short periods. All members of the pack help carry the babies. AGE EXPECTATION (LIFE SPAN) About 10 years in the wild. Up to 17 years in captivity. FUN FACT Banded mongooses may travel over 8 km (5 mi.) a day when foraging for food. CONSERVATION At this point in time, the banded mongoose is widespread in its native habitat. There are no threats to this species currently.

The Fable of Secretary Bird, Mongoose, and Snake

Long ago, Secretary Bird and Mongoose were good friends. They were walking in the bush when they met a large snake. Snake asked Mongoose to join him because he had something special to show him. Secretary Bird headed off on her own. After walking for a long time, Snake and Mongoose came upon a nest full of eggs. Snake knew these were Secretary Bird's eggs but did not say, so Mongoose and Snake ate the eggs. Secretary Bird arrived and was sad and angry. Mongoose told her that Snake had tricked him into eating the eggs. Mongoose and Secretary Bird killed Snake and watched out for snakes from then on.

Able to race as fast as speedy cars, cheetahs are fierce and fast predators.

Cheetah

It is a hot morning in the grasslands of Kenya. The sky is bright blue and there is not a cloud in sight. A female cheetah rests in the tall grass along with her three cubs. She is hungry. From her grassy hideout, she scans her surroundings in search of prey. Her eyesight is excellent. After a few minutes, the cheetah spies an impala. The impala is still in the distance, grazing on grass. The cheetah waits for it to move a bit closer. When she feels the impala is within striking distance, she dashes out of her hiding spot. Her spots are practically a blur as she whizzes through the grass. The impala tries to sprint away from the cheetah. But no land animal can match the cheetah's speed. Sometimes cheetahs can race up to 113 km/h (70 mph) over a short distance. But in this case, that type of speed was not necessary. The cheetah quickly catches up with the impala. She uses her strong, curved dewclaw to hook her prey. The impala is thrown off balance. The cheetah wastes no time in knocking it to the ground. The cheetah grabs the impala by the throat then bites down hard. This fierce feline maintains its stranglehold on the impala. Within minutes, the prey stops twitching and is dead.

The cheetah drags its prey into a shady spot. She is panting hard after the hunt. She rests for nearly 30 minutes, catching her breath after the speedy chase. Then she and her cubs eat heartily. The cheetah's superpower is speed—and it won her a feast!

Fact File

SCIENTIFIC NAME *Acinonyx jubatus* (cheetah) CLASS Mammalia (mammal) HEIGHT 0.8–0.9 m (2.6–3.0 ft.) at the shoulder LENGTH 1.8–2.4 m (6–8 ft.). The tail is about half as long as a cheetah's head and body. WEIGHT 35–65 kg (77–143 lb.). At birth, a cheetah weighs 150–300 g (5–11 oz.) HABITAT Grasslands, savannahs, open woodlands, semi-desert areas LOCATION Cheetahs live in eastern, central, and southern Africa. They are most common in Kenya, Tanzania, and Namibia/southwestern Africa. A few hundred cheetahs live in the Sahara Desert. NUTRITION Cheetahs are carnivores (meat-eaters). They tend to eat small to medium-sized animals like impalas, hares, gazelles, and wildebeest calves. Cheetah cubs nurse on their mother's milk for around three and a half months but start eating meat at around five weeks old. SOCIAL BEHAVIOR Female cheetahs tend to live on their own or with their dependent young. Males either live alone or in small groups of two or three individuals. Adult males and females interact only briefly during mating season. Cheetahs normally hunt during the daytime and rest at night. FAMILY + OFFSPRING The gestation period of cheetahs is about 90–95 days. On average, a cheetah mother gives birth to three or four cubs. They give birth in a hidden den, often under a thorn bush or in long, thick grass. Females raise their young on their own. Cheetah cubs typically leave their mothers between 14–18 months old. AGE EXPECTATION (LIFE SPAN) 10–12 years FUN FACT Cheetahs cannot roar but they can purr—both when inhaling and exhaling! PHYSICAL DESCRIPTION Cheetahs have very slender bodies and tall, thin legs. Usually the background of their coat is a tan or yellow color. Solid black dots are evenly spaced on their pelt. The heads of cheetahs are small. Their eyes are set high on their heads and their ears are small and flattened. CONSERVATION Cheetahs are endangered. There are estimated to be about 9,000–12,000 cheetahs living in the wild in Africa today. Habitat loss is a problem for cheetahs. Their grassland homes are often destroyed by agriculture, roads, and human settlements. Sometimes farmers kill cheetahs when these cats attack their livestock.

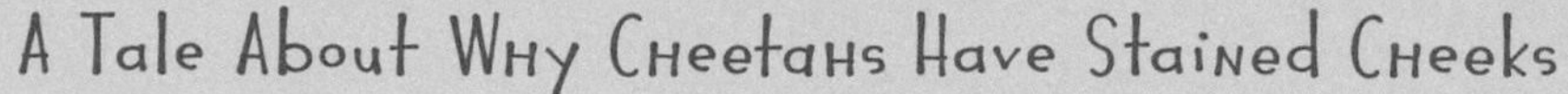

A Tale About Why Cheetahs Have Stained Cheeks

Long ago, a lazy hunter sat under a tree. He watched as a female cheetah hunted for food for her three cubs. He was jealous of the cubs as they had great food without having to hunt themselves. Later the mother cheetah went to the waterhole alone. The wicked hunter stole her three cubs, hoping he could train them to hunt for him. When the mother cheetah returned, she was heartbroken. She cried so much that her tears made dark stains down both her cheeks. The villagers chased the hunter away. An old man returned the cheetah cubs to their mother. But to this day, cheetahs wear the tear stains on their faces.

Cheetah
–
The speedy exit of a
cheetah from the tall grass
causes a flock of birds to
quickly take flight.

Spectacular swimmers with bone-crushing jaws,
Nile crocodiles can sneak up on prey—human or animal.

Nile Crocodile

It is just after dusk in a river in eastern Africa. Time for a Nile crocodile to start thinking about food. This crocodile is huge—about five meters (16 ft.) long—with tough, bumpy skin. It is on the prowl.

Submerged in the river, the fearsome predator patrols the water while keeping his eyes just above the surface. He is great at sneaking up on an unsuspecting animal—or human. The Nile crocodile has earned its reputation as a man-eater. Some estimates say that these creatures kill as many as 200 people per year.

A group of thirsty wildebeests arrives at the river's edge. The crocodile sets his sights on one. He closes his eyes and submerges himself completely. With his webbed hind feet, he swims quickly. Pressure receptors on his jaw sense vibrations made by the wildebeest. Suddenly—splash! The crocodile uses his muscular tail to propel himself out of the water.

Lightning-fast, the crocodile grabs his prey by the throat. Holding onto the wildebeest with his bone-crushing jaws, the croc drags it into the water. He has scored a delicious dinner!

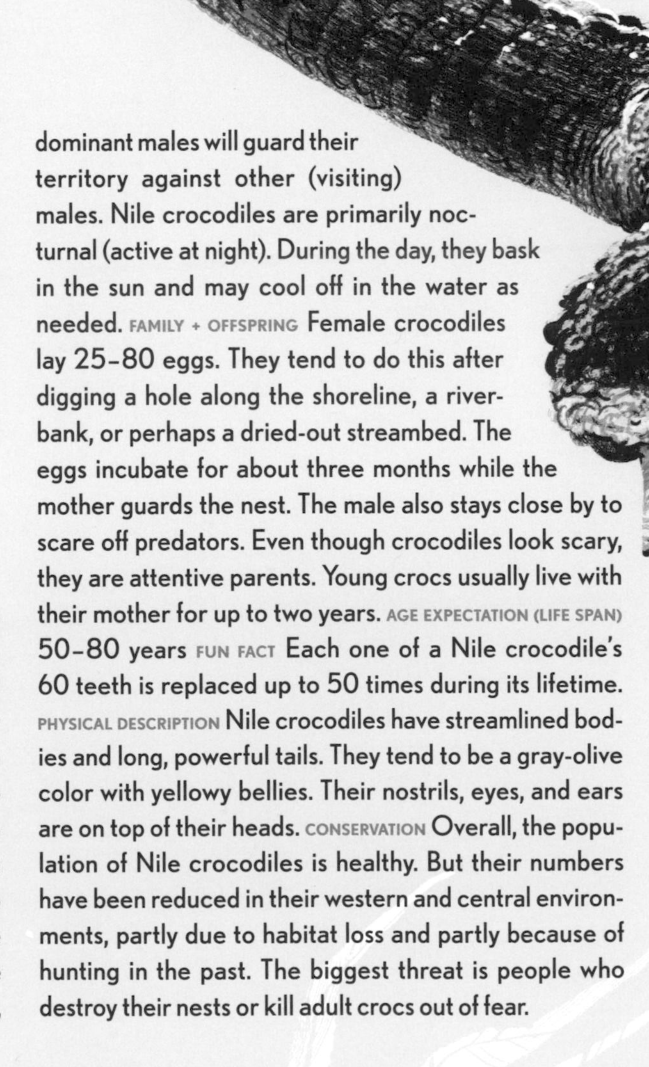

Fact File

SCIENTIFIC NAME *Crocodylus niloticus* (Nile crocodile) CLASS Reptilia (reptiles) LENGTH 2–3.3 m (7–11 ft.) for body, 5 meters (16 ft.) is the maximum length from snout to end of tail. WEIGHT 70–100 kg (154–220 lb.) HABITAT Freshwater rivers and lakes; some brackish coastal swamps LOCATION Nile crocodiles are native to Madagascar. But they are widely found south of the Sahara in Africa. NUTRITION Nile crocodiles are carnivores (meat-eaters). Hatchlings eat insects and small fish. Adults eat prey from impala to young hippos and lions. SOCIAL BEHAVIOR Nile crocodiles are highly social animals. They are often seen basking in the sun in large groups. However, during breeding season, dominant males will guard their territory against other (visiting) males. Nile crocodiles are primarily nocturnal (active at night). During the day, they bask in the sun and may cool off in the water as needed. FAMILY + OFFSPRING Female crocodiles lay 25–80 eggs. They tend to do this after digging a hole along the shoreline, a riverbank, or perhaps a dried-out streambed. The eggs incubate for about three months while the mother guards the nest. The male also stays close by to scare off predators. Even though crocodiles look scary, they are attentive parents. Young crocs usually live with their mother for up to two years. AGE EXPECTATION (LIFE SPAN) 50–80 years FUN FACT Each one of a Nile crocodile's 60 teeth is replaced up to 50 times during its lifetime. PHYSICAL DESCRIPTION Nile crocodiles have streamlined bodies and long, powerful tails. They tend to be a gray-olive color with yellowy bellies. Their nostrils, eyes, and ears are on top of their heads. CONSERVATION Overall, the population of Nile crocodiles is healthy. But their numbers have been reduced in their western and central environments, partly due to habitat loss and partly because of hunting in the past. The biggest threat is people who destroy their nests or kill adult crocs out of fear.

The Fable of Hen and Crocodile

Day after day, Hen went to look for food down by the river. One day Crocodile saw her. He opened his mouth wide and threatened to eat her. Hen replied, "Don't eat me, my brother." She was not afraid. Crocodile snapped his mouth shut. He could not eat her. This happened several times. Finally, Crocodile asked the wise old woman how he could be Hen's brother. She told Crocodile that scales and feathers did not matter. Both crocodiles and chickens lay eggs. And from then on Crocodile treated Hen like a sister.

Thriving in colonies, both of these ants have special techniques to avoid or scare off predators in the wild.

Saharan Silver Ant

It is midday in the Sahara Desert. The air temperature is more than 50°C (122°F). And the sand is scorching—it can reach 65–70°C (149–158°F)! Many insects and animals in the Sahara stay out of sight during this time. But not the Saharan silver ant. This ant has superpowers when it comes to beating the heat! Here are just a couple of them: these ants are coated in silver hair that reflects light and protects them from the sun's heat. And they have longer legs than other ants that allow their bodies to be elevated above the hot sand. These legs also let the ants run really fast, making it easier to stay cool. They never get lost: these ants are great at navigating and can always find the shortest route back home to their nest.

SCIENTIFIC NAME *Cataglyphis bombycina* (Saharan silver ant) **CLASS** Insecta (insects) **HABITAT** Desert **LOCATION** Sahara Desert **NUTRITION** These ants eat insects (mostly flies). Many of the insects they eat have died from heat stress. **SOCIAL BEHAVIOR** Scouts keep watch and let the colony know when ant lizards (a major predator) go for shelter in their burrows. Then the Saharan silver ants head out to find food. **FUN FACT** Saharan silver ants can withstand body temperatures up to about 52.7°C (127°F)!

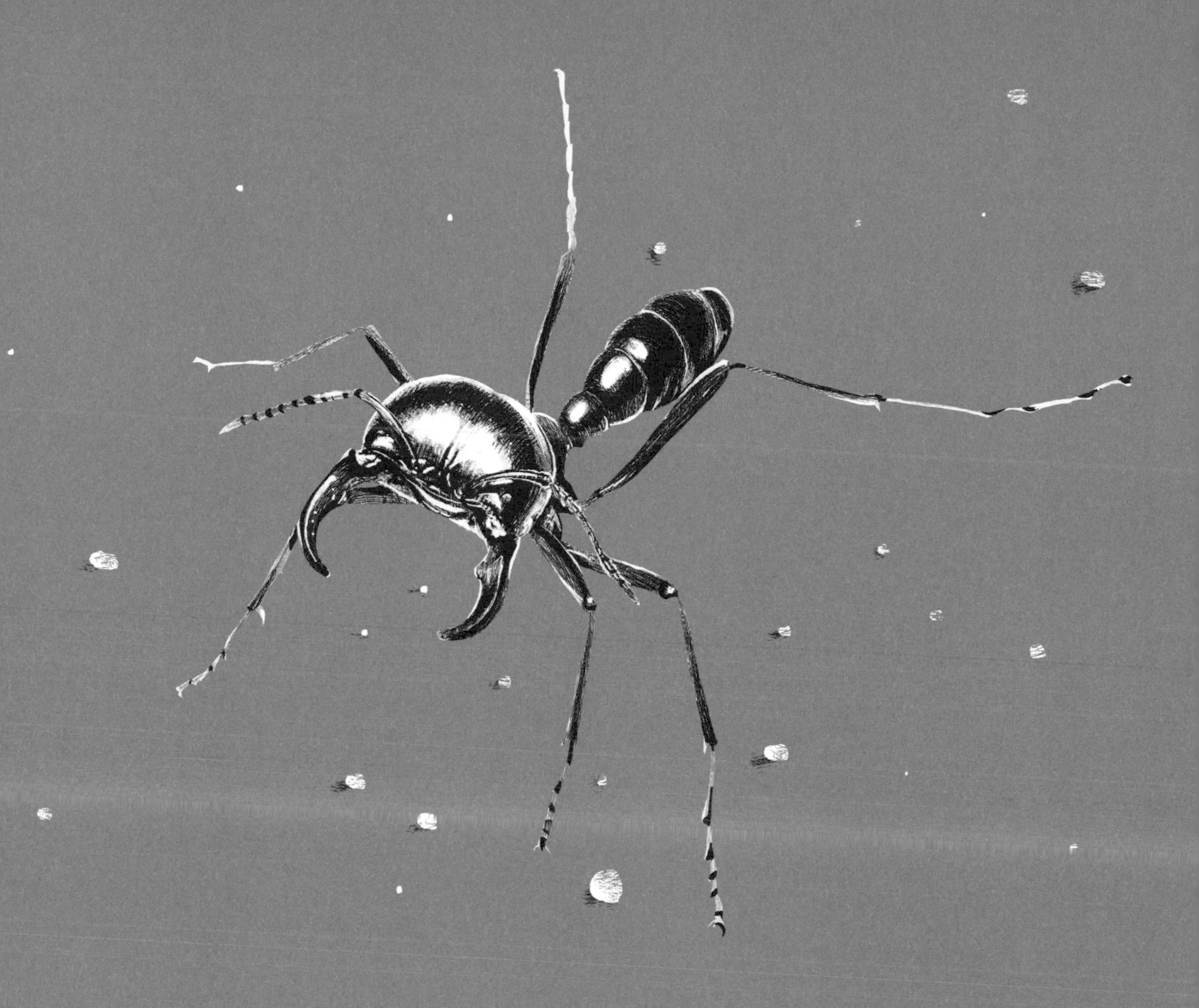

Matabele Ants

Matabele ants are serious termite killers. They often attack the termites in raiding columns of as many as 1,000 individuals. The Matabele ants dig into the termite tunnels then capture, sting, and drag the termites to the surface. After killing its prey, a single Matabele ant can carry 12 termites back to its nest at a time!

SCIENTIFIC NAME *Pachycondyla analis* (matabele ants) CLASS Insecta (insects) LENGTH 9–11 mm (0.35–0.45 in.) for minor workers, up to 15 mm (0.59 in.) for major workers HABITAT Savannahs and tropical dry forests LOCATION Matabele ants live south of the Sahara. NUTRITION Matabele ants feed almost exclusively on termites. SOCIAL BEHAVIOR Matabele ants typically live in colonies of between 400 and 1,400 members. One queen is responsible for the whole colony's reproduction. FUN FACT These ants are named after the Matabele people of western Zimbabwe, who are known for being excellent warriors.

The spines of the lowland streaked tenrec can be used to communicate...or to pierce predators. Ouch!

Lowland Streaked Tenrec

It is a hot day in the rainforest of eastern Madagascar. Birds are calling from the trees above. Leaves of every shade of green are all around. A lowland streaked tenrec wanders around on the forest floor. It is looking for earthworms or perhaps some other tasty invertebrates. It finds a worm and pulls it from the soil below with its long snout. Yum!

Moments later, the tenrec hears something. It sounds like an animal is coming closer. It is a Malagasy ring-tailed mongoose, a predator. Time for this tenrec to use its superpower—spines! First the tenrec uses its stridulation organ, which is made up of specialized spines. When these spines rub together, they make a noise that some think warns off predators.

Unfortunately, the mongoose is not scared off. It continues to pursue the tenrec. The lowland streaked tenrec stamps its feet. It makes chattering sounds. The mongoose gets closer still. Now the tenrec is mad. It rushes to head-butt the attacking mongoose. Bam! Some of the tenrec's head spines are dislodged. These barbed spines dig into the flesh of the mongoose. Ouch!

The mongoose is in pain and tries to remove the painful quills from its skin. While the Malagasy mongoose tries to deal with its injuries, the much smaller lowland streaked tenrec makes a speedy getaway. Its quills have saved its life!

Fact File

SCIENTIFIC NAME *Hemicentetes semispinosus* (lowland streaked tenrec) CLASS Mammalia (mammal) LENGTH Up to 19 cm (7 in.) WEIGHT 125–180 g (4–6 oz.) HABITAT Tropical rainforest LOCATION Lowland streaked tenrecs only live on the island of Madagascar. NUTRITION Lowland streaked tenrecs mainly eat worms, though they also eat other invertebrates with soft bodies and insects. Young tenrecs nurse on their mother's milk for around 25 days. SOCIAL BEHAVIOR Lowland streaked tenrecs live in family groups of up to 20 individuals. They nest in burrows, usually near a body of water. These animals are mainly active during the day. FAMILY + OFFSPRING The gestation period of lowland streaked tenrecs is about 55–58 days. Females can give birth to as many as eleven offspring, though six is an average litter size. They typically clear a depression in the ground for giving birth. Males let their young huddle around them for protection. Females will carry their offspring back to their nest if they wander too far away. Mothers and their babies communicate by vibrating special quills found in the middle of their backs that create a high-pitched noise. AGE EXPECTATION (LIFE SPAN) 30 months (in captivity) FUN FACT Lowland streaked tenrecs are born without spines but begin to develop them within 24 hours of being born. PHYSICAL DESCRIPTION These unusual-looking animals are covered in black and yellow quills. They look somewhat like a cross between a hedgehog and a shrew with their pointed, long snouts. CONSERVATION The greatest threat to lowland streaked tenrecs is habitat loss. This is often caused by deforestation. Tenrecs can also be disturbed by tourists on the island of Madagascar. Conservation of forest habitats on the island will help maintain the survival of these unique animals.

Madagascan Myths

In northeastern and central Madagascar, it is forbidden to consume the lowland streaked tenrec. Why? Many people here believe that these animals helped to protect their ancestors from enemies during dangerous times such as war.

They shed strips of skin in an attack, they take dust baths...these rodents are some of the most interesting in Africa.

Kemp's Spiny Mouse

In the dry savannah of East Africa, many animals prey on mice. And Kemp's spiny mouse is no exception. While out looking for food, a predator may try to grab this mouse. But the Kemp's spiny mouse has a superpower. It can release strips of skin from its back. That way, the predator just takes away a chunk of the mouse rather than its whole body. It sounds gross, but this amazing mouse can lose as much as 60 percent of the skin off its back—and survive.

Kemp's spiny mouse has crazy powers of healing. After being attacked by a predator, this mouse's wounds shrink dramatically within 24 hours. It can completely regrow enough skin to cover the wound in just three days. And the new tissue resembles just what it had been before the injury occurred. Good as new, so to speak!

SCIENTIFIC NAME *Acomys kempi* (Kemp's spiny mouse) CLASS Mammalia (mammals) LENGTH 95–110 mm (3.5–4.3 in.) for head and body, 82–106 mm (3.2–4.2 in.) for tail WEIGHT 30–40 g (1.0–1.4 oz.) HABITAT Rocky areas in the dry savannah and semi-desert LOCATION East Africa—specifically Ethiopia, Somalia, Kenya, and Tanzania NUTRITION Kemp's spiny mouse eats insects. SOCIAL BEHAVIOR Not much is known about the social behavior of these mice in the wild. In captivity, they tend to spend a considerable amount of time in small groups. The groups are made up of one or two males, several females, and their offspring. FAMILY + OFFSPRING The gestation period for Kemp's spiny mouse is about 38 to 42 days. Females may have as many as six pups in a litter. Females that are not the mothers will also tend to newborn pups.

Short-eared Elephant Shrew

There is an African folktale about why the elephant shrew has a long snout. Once upon a time, Warthog, Nightjar, and Elephant Shrew were walking together. At that time Warthog had a long nose. Nightjar had a tiny mouth. And Elephant Shrew had a small, snub snout. Warthog saw a beehive in a tree. He climbed the tree and knocked the hive to the ground. He leaned too far and fell over, squashing his nose flat. Nightjar found this so funny that he laughed and laughed. His mouth split wider and wider. Elephant Shrew did not want this to happen to him. He pushed his lips forward, trying to stifle his laugh. Instead, his snout grew as long as it is today.

SCIENTIFIC NAME *Macroscelides proboscideus* (short-eared elephant shrew) CLASS Mammalia (mammals) LENGTH 10 cm (4 in.) for body WEIGHT 28–43 g (1.0–1.5 oz.) HABITAT Short-eared elephant shrews like to live in habitats where they are able to burrow into sandy soil. These habitats include dry semi-desert, shrub land, or dry grass. LOCATION Southern Africa—Namibia, Botswana, and South Africa NUTRITION Short-eared elephant shrews are omnivores. They eat termites, ants, berries and the shoots of young plants. SOCIAL BEHAVIOR These shrews are largely solitary animals. Adults spend most of their lives on their own, except for when mating. Short-eared elephant shrews are diurnal (active during the day). FAMILY + OFFSPRING The gestation period for short-eared elephant shrews is 56 days. Females usually give birth to a litter of one or two. Offspring start hunting at two weeks old. They look for their own home habitat at around five to six weeks of age. AGE EXPECTATION (LIFE SPAN) 1–2 years (in the wild) 3–4 years (in captivity) FUN FACT These shrews clean themselves by taking dust baths!

Tool builders and power nappers, these animals are some of the smartest in their rainforest home.

Western Lowland Gorilla

A troop of western lowland gorillas is gathering food in the dense rainforest of western Africa. It is a sunny day. The weather is hot and humid. One of the troop members climbs a tree in search of ripe fruit to eat. Another feasts on herbs and leaves. As the gorillas wander about their forest home, they come upon a pool of water. How deep is it? One of the troop's female members uses her superpower—intelligence—to find out.

The female grabs a nearby branch from a fallen tree. She uses the branch for two purposes. First, she puts the branch into the water to determine its depth. Then, deciding it is not too deep to cross, she uses the branch again. This time she uses it like a walking stick to help her wade through the pool more easily. She repeatedly prods the stick into the water in front of her as she crosses the pool. After about 10 m (33 ft.), she has made it across and leaves her walking stick behind.

Several other members of the troop cross the pool, following in the footsteps of this clever female. One of the males has found an ant hole. He sticks his hand into the hole to extract the ants but—ouch! They start biting him. The gorilla does not give up. Instead he finds a nearby stick. He plunges the stick into the hole, which comes out of the ground covered in ants. Chomp! The gorilla's tool use was a success. He got to eat but avoided getting bitten.

Fact File

SCIENTIFIC NAME *Gorilla gorilla gorilla* (western lowland gorilla) **CLASS** Mammalia (mammals) **HEIGHT** Up to 1.5 m (4.9 ft.) for females, up to 1.75 m (5.7 ft.) for males **WEIGHT** 72–98 kg (159–216 lb.) for females, 136–181 kg (300–400 lb.) for males, 1.8–2.3 kg (4–5 lb.) at birth **HABITAT** Rain forests **LOCATION** Western lowland gorillas live in west and central Africa. **NUTRITION** Western lowland gorillas are omnivores. Gorillas mainly eat plants, but they also eat ants and termites. Gorillas may nurse for as long as three years. **SOCIAL BEHAVIOR** Gorillas are social creatures. A group of gorillas that lives together is known as a troop. One troop can have between five and 30 members. A "silverback" male leads the troop and is responsible for the members' well-being and safety. **FAMILY + OFFSPRING** Female gorillas are ready to have babies at around eight years old. Before having babies, females leave their own troop to live with another troop or a lone silverback. Gestation is eight to nine months. Females usually give birth to one baby. Gorilla mothers carry their babies against their chest for several months until they are able to hold onto her back. Young gorillas share their mom's nest for four to six years. **AGE EXPECTATION (LIFE SPAN)** 35 years in the wild **FUN FACT** An adult male eats as much as 18 kg (40 lb.) of food each day! **CONSERVATION** The population of gorillas has declined dramatically in recent decades. Illegal hunting is one threat to these animals. So is the illegal pet trade. Logging and mining companies have also destroyed some of the gorillas' natural habitats.

The Tale of Gorilla and Chimpanzee

A great hunter was determined to kill Gorilla. Gorilla had been damaging his plantation. After traveling far, the hunter found Gorilla's camp. Gorilla was up a tree, but at the base of the tree was a huge pile of fruits. Chimpanzee showed up and started eating the fruit. Gorilla came down the tree and started eating the fruit, too. Chimpanzee asked Gorilla to find his own fruit. Chimpanzee shouted at Gorilla and hit him with his hand. Gorilla smiled and pushed Chimpanzee away. Chimpanzee hit Gorilla with a club. Gorilla struck Chimpanzee with one blow and Chimpanzee was dead.The hunter ran away.

Despite their small size, these insects can easily outwit and kill their prey.

Ant Lion

Below the soft, sandy soil of South Africa hides a small but incredible predator: a larva of an ant lion. This tiny creature is no larger than a human fingernail and yet it is a shockingly effective killer. The ant lion larva forms a cone-shaped hole with smooth sides in the sandy soil. It uses its mandibles (sickle-like jaws) to flick the sand away until this trap is just right.

When any tiny walking insect comes into the hole, the ant lion larva shoots grains of sand at it. This causes the prey to slide toward the bottom of its hole. Then the ant lion larva pulls its victim underground. Even though an ant lion larva does not have a mouth that opens and closes, it grabs its prey using its mandibles. The ant lion stabs its victim, injects it with digestive enzymes, and sucks out the soft tissues from inside its body for a liquid meal. Then the ant lion larva tosses the empty body of its prey onto the edge of the trap. Eventually, the piles of dead insects grow larger. It is like a bug graveyard!

SCIENTIFIC NAME *Myrmeleo* (ant lion) CLASS Insecta (insects) LENGTH Ant lions come in different sizes, but well nourished larvae can be 1.2 cm (0.5 in.) long. The wingspan of adult ant lions can range from less than 4 up to 16 cm (2–6 in.). HABITAT Ant lions often live in dry and sandy habitats. LOCATION There are more than 2,000 species of ant lions around the world. They are common in the deserts of Africa, North America, and Australia. NUTRITION Ant lions are insectivores (insect-eaters) as larvae but often feed on pollen and nectar as adults. AGE EXPECTATION (LIFE SPAN) The average lifespan of an adult ant lion is about 20 to 25 days. FUN FACT Ant lions are also known as "doodlebugs" because of the trail of loose sand or soil that they leave in their wake.

Bombardier Beetle

The bombardier beetle looks small but it has incredible defensive powers. The body of this amazing insect has some hidden strengths. This beetle is able to fire a powerful jet of fluid at its enemies. But this is no ordinary fluid—it is very hot and very toxic. The African bombardier beetle can spray its toxic liquid in just about any direction and hit its target with great accuracy. The liquid can squirt out up to 20 cm (8 in.) from the beetle's body. How does the bombardier beetle's toxin work? Inside the insect's body is a special chamber known as the "firing chamber." When the beetle is alarmed or a predator approaches, a special valve opens. Then the hydrogen peroxide gases and a chemical compound called hydroquinone are mixed together. The resulting liquid is very irritating to predators and comes out of the beetle's body at 100°C (212°F)! The hot and nasty toxin is fired off—with a loud "pop"—into the faces of predators like frogs or birds. Beware of the bombardier beetle's back end!

SCIENTIFIC NAME *Stenaptinus insignis* (African bombardier beetle, bull's-eye beetle) CLASS Insecta (insects) LENGTH About 20 mm (0.8 in.) HABITAT Bombardier beetles often live under rocks, loose bark, or on the ground out in the open at night. They can often be found near floodplains or by the edges of temporary ponds. LOCATION This species of bombardier beetle is from sub-Saharan Africa. NUTRITION These beetles are carnivores and hunt for insects at night. AGE EXPECTATION (LIFE SPAN) Over a year FUN FACT Charles Darwin once put a bombardier beetle in his mouth, but its nasty fluid burned his tongue so he had to spit it out!

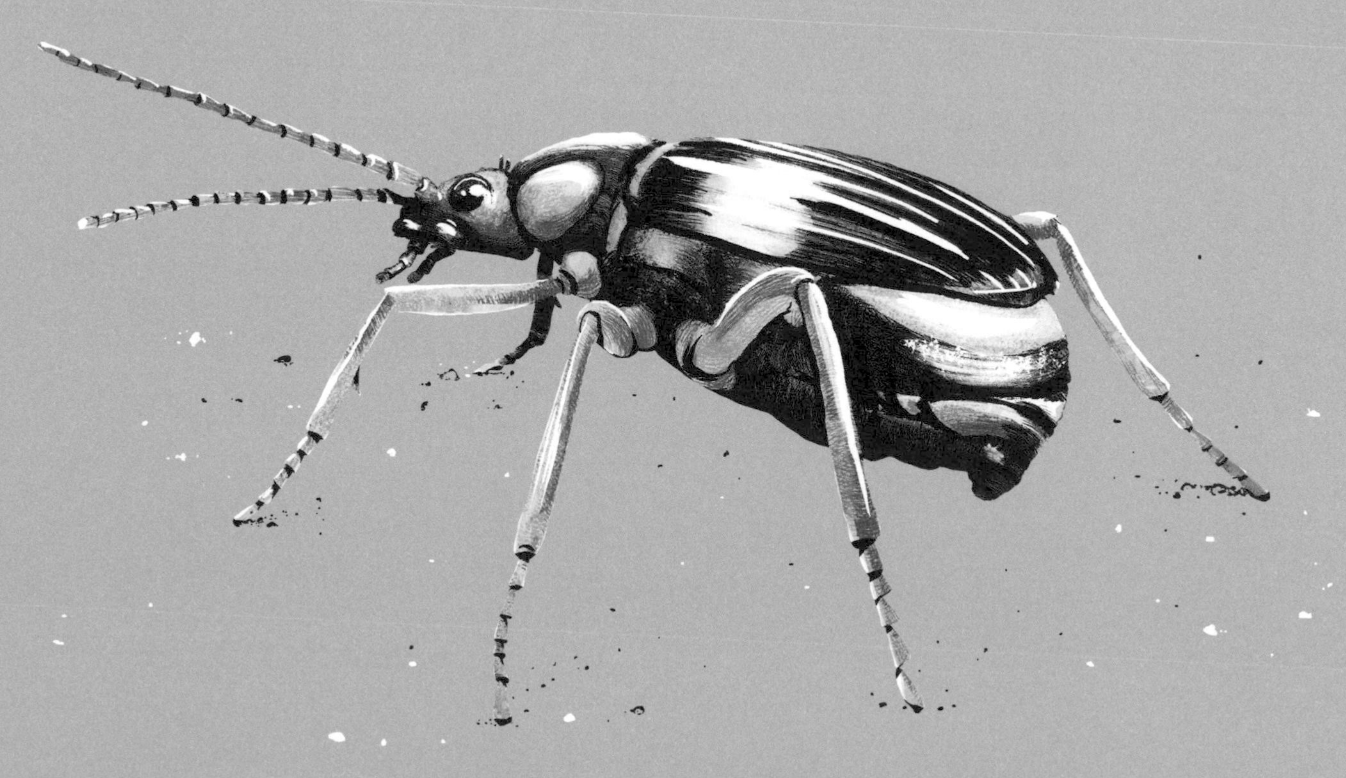

Built for digging, aardvarks use their long, sticky tongues to slurp thousands of insects each night.

Aardvark

In the cool of the evening, an aardvark emerges from its underground burrow. Its snout is long, almost like that of a pig. In fact, aardvark means "earth pig" in the Afrikaans language of South Africa. This animal is on the move. It is searching for dinner. What is on the menu tonight? Termites.

The aardvark forages in its grassland home. While this odd-looking creature has poor eyesight, it has other advantages. For one thing, its claws look like small digging spades. The aardvark comes upon a termite mound. It quickly dismantles the earthen mound, tearing it apart with its claws. Slurp! The aardvark is like a living termite vacuum. Its sticky tongue darts out, catching loads of termites. In fact, an aardvark can eat as many as 50,000 insects in a single night—talk about a feeding frenzy!

Aardvarks do not chew their food. Instead, they just swallow it whole. Luckily for the aardvark, it has some special features to protect it while it eats. Aardvarks can close their nostrils so insects and dust do not go inside. And their thick skin protects them from the bites of their prey. This is very helpful when swarming termites crawl all over the face and head of their destructive predator.

Aardvarks are amazing. They are incredible diggers and suctioning, slurping superheroes. Insects like ants and termites do not stand a chance when aardvarks arrive on the scene!

Fact File

SCIENTIFIC NAME *Orycteropus afer* (Aardvark, ant bear) CLASS Mammalia (mammals) HEIGHT 61 cm (24 in.) at the shoulder LENGTH 109.2–134.6 cm (43–53 in.) for body, 53.3–66 cm (21–26 in.) for tail WEIGHT 49.9–81.6 kg (110–180 lb.), 2 kg (4 lb.) at birth HABITAT Aardvarks can live in many different habitats, such as savannahs, grasslands, rainforests, and woodlands. LOCATION Africa, south of the Sahara NUTRITION Aardvarks are carnivores (meat-eaters). The main foods they eat are ants and termites. Young aardvarks are weaned at about three months old. SOCIAL BEHAVIOR Aardvarks are generally solitary creatures. They come together to mate but are on their own otherwise. Aardvarks are nocturnal (active at night). During the hot afternoons, they keep cool in their underground burrows. FAMILY + OFFSPRING The gestation period for aardvarks is seven months. Females usually give birth to one offspring each year. Young aardvarks stay with their mothers for about six months and then go off to dig their own burrows. AGE EXPECTATION (LIFE SPAN) Up to 23 years in captivity FUN FACT An aardvark's tongue can be up to 30.5 cm (12 in.) long! PHYSICAL DESCRIPTION Aardvarks are strange looking animals. They have long snouts, ears like a rabbit, and a tail like a kangaroo. CONSERVATION Aardvarks are not a threatened or endangered species. However, their populations in some areas of Africa are decreasing due to hunting and human population growth. TRIBAL INFORMATION In some African cultures, traditional healers use the bone of the aardvark as a medical treatment for backaches. And the feces (poop) of an aardvark is used for medicinal purposes among the Setswana people of Botswana.

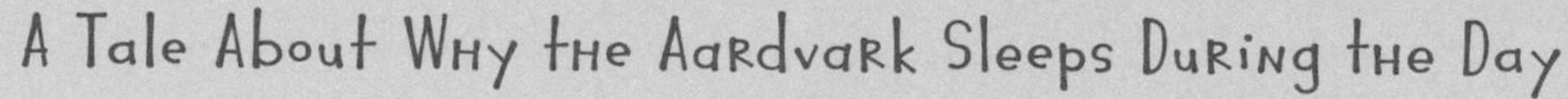

Every night Aardvark slept in his favorite tree. Night after night he snored loudly. So loudly that he kept Mongoose and the other animals awake. Mongoose came up with an idea, and met with Lion, Monkey, and Rhinoceros. That evening Aardvark was snoring as usual. The animals all tried to wake him. First the monkeys screeched. Then Lion scratched the bark of his tree. Then Rhinoceros bumped into the tree. But after each time Aardvark fell asleep again and started snoring. Eventually, there was a munching sound near the roots of Aardvark's tree. Crash! The tree fell over and Aardvark hit the ground. He slurped up the termites who had toppled his tree. From that night on, Aardvark slept in the day and ate termites at night.

With superhero-like appetites, desert locusts can ruin crops—or be eaten as snacks by humans.

Desert Locust

It is a sunny day in the central Sahara. Unusual rains have hit in recent weeks, causing vegetation to grow and life to flourish. The desert locusts take full advantage of the increase in water and green plant life. These amazing but devastating creatures are like superheroes under these ideal conditions. They grow fast, eat lots, and take over whatever landscape they cross.

Eggs that have been in the ground for 20 years suddenly start to hatch. These young desert locusts are called hoppers because they cannot fly yet. They simply follow the scent of sprouting grass. Adult locusts descend on any vegetation they happen upon. Swarms of these insects can devour entire fields in a short time. Once the food is gone, the locusts release pheromones to let others know it is time to move on.

Adult desert locusts eat their weight in food each day. So it does not take long for a swarm to consume hundreds of tons of plant life. Just a small swarm (about one ton of locusts) can eat as much in one day as about 25 camels or 2,500 humans! They basically eat every edible plant in their path.

Luckily for the people in Africa, desert locusts do not swarm every year. These locusts can ruin all the crops in an area, causing severe hardship and food shortages for people. When two or more regions are affected by swarms of locusts, it is called a plague. The last such plague happened in 1987–1989. One thing is for sure—desert locusts have appetites worthy of superheroes.

Fact File

SCIENTIFIC NAME *Schistocerca gregaria* (desert locust) CLASS Insecta (insect) LENGTH 1.2–7.5 cm (0.5–3.0 in.) WEIGHT 2 g (0.07 oz.) HABITAT Farmland, desert, tropical grassland, mountain grassland LOCATION Africa, the Middle East, and Asia. Normally these insects live in the central Sahara, the Arabian Peninsula, and Persian Gulf regions. But when conditions are right, they travel as far north as Russia and Spain and even the Caribbean. NUTRITION Desert locusts are herbivores (plant-eaters). SOCIAL BEHAVIOR Sometimes locusts are solitary creatures, living lives similar to their grasshopper relatives. But they also have a time known as the gregarious phase. This is when locusts gather together into hungry, thick swarms that are on the move. FAMILY + OFFSPRING Female desert locusts lay eggs in something called an egg pod, usually in sandy soils around 10–15 cm (4-6 in.) below the surface. A solitary female typically lays between 95 and 158 eggs, but a gregarious female usually lays less than 80 eggs. Incubation of the eggs can take different lengths of time depending on the soil temperature, varying between 10 and 70 days. AGE EXPECTATION (LIFE SPAN) 3–5 months FUN FACT Between 40 and 80 million locusts can swarm into an area of one square kilometer (0.4 sq. mi.)!

Eating Locusts

People in many different countries eat these insects. A Tswana recipe calls for the cook to remove the locust's hind legs and wings, boil the locust in water, and add salt, if they like, before frying it until brown. The Swazi people prepare locusts by roasting them whole in the embers of a fire. Some people dry locusts for the winter months, finding the dried legs to be especially tasty.

Desert Locust
–
As the locusts eat their way through the plants in this area, other animals head for different locations.

With their unbelievable jumping skills, servals can catch prey in mid-air.

Serval

The sky is starting to darken on the African savannah. A serval rises from its resting spot amidst the grass. With its long legs, the cat is able to see over the savannah's grasses. It makes sure no predators are nearby. The serval is thirsty. It makes its way over to a waterhole. After drinking its fill, the serval uses its claws to hook a frog right out of the water. Chomp! A tasty morsel to start the evening's meal. Last night the serval caught a fish in a stream not far from here.

The air is full of many different bird calls. Many of them are heading back to their nests to settle down for the night. To the serval, these birds are flying food. Servals are patient hunters. They walk slowly through the grasslands, stopping to listen from time to time.

The serval waits and then uses its superpower. It leaps three meters (10 ft.) into the air! All four of its paws are off the ground in what is known as a capriole jump. With its front paws, the serval holds onto its prey. The bird cannot escape. The serval lands with its back feet on the ground and devours the bird.

The frog and the bird were good to eat but the serval is still hungry. Nighttime is a great time to catch rodents that are on the move. The serval hears something moving in the grass. It could be a grass mouse or a vlei rat. Again, the serval pauses and listens. This cat uses its fantastic hearing to determine exactly where the rodent is. The serval pounces—more than 3.5 m (11 ft.) in one pounce—and again catches its prey. After a death bite to the neck, the serval eats the rat. Being an amazing jumper keeps the serval well fed!

Fact File

SCIENTIFIC NAME *Leptailurus serval* (serval) **CLASS** Mammalia (mammals) **HEIGHT** 45–60 cm (18–24 in.) tall at the shoulder **LENGTH** 59–92 cm (23–36 in.) **WEIGHT** 7–18 kg (15–40 lb.), 227–255 g (8–9 oz.) at birth **HABITAT** Savannahs where there is plenty of water **LOCATION** Central and southern Africa **NUTRITION** Servals are carnivores (meat-eaters). They eat birds, frogs, reptiles, large insects, and crabs. **SOCIAL BEHAVIOR** Male and female servals live separately for most of the year, except during breeding season. For the most part, servals are solitary animals, though males sometimes rest together in small groups during the day. **FAMILY + OFFSPRING** The gestation period for servals is 70 to 79 days. Females give birth to between one and five offspring, but usually they have three in a litter. Females raise their kittens on their own. Kittens usually live in a den made from thick grass or even a burrow that has been abandoned. Male kittens stay with their mothers for about six months, while female kittens may remain with their mothers for about two years. **AGE EXPECTATION (LIFE SPAN)** Up to 19 years **FUN FACT** For their body size, servals have the largest ears and longest legs of any cat. **PHYSICAL DESCRIPTION** Servals have long legs and long necks. They are medium-sized wild cats. They have tawny fur with black spots. **CONSERVATION** The major threat to servals is habitat loss through the degradation of wetlands, which are an important part of these cats' habitats. Another threat is the burning of grasslands and over-grazing of livestock in areas where servals live. Sometimes humans kill these cats because servals prey on their poultry.

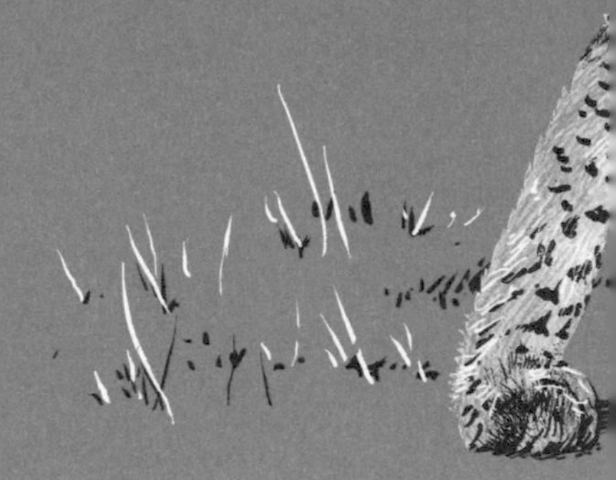

A Tale About Why Servals Have Spots

In the beginning, Serval was the same color as Lion. But Serval was much smaller and weaker. The other animals teased him. They called him Lion's small Cousin. Serval wished for a beautiful coat like Zebra or Leopard. While out hunting, Serval met Puff Adder. Adder was feeling quite ill and asked Serval for help. Serval agreed to help if Adder promised not to bite him. Serval took care of Adder until he was well. Adder offered to do anything he could in return for Serval's kindness. Serval asked for a beautiful coat. Adder said he could bite Serval with just a little poison. After the bite, Serval broke out in a rash—and after that his goldon coat was dotted with black spots.

Expert jumpers and chemical communicators, these insects thrive in colonies.

Trap-jaw Ant

Have you ever seen a trap-jaw ant? They are a bit scary looking with their oversized jaws. When a trap-jaw ant hunts, these jaws strike fast—easily crushing or taking the limbs off of prey. In fact, these insects have some of the animal kingdom's fastest jaws. Not bad for a tiny insect!

SCIENTIFIC NAME *Odontomachus coquereli* (trap-jaw ant) CLASS Insecta (insects) HABITAT Rainforest and littoral forest. These trap-jaw ants are often found in rotten logs. LOCATION These trap-jaw ants are only found on Madagascar. NUTRITION Trap-jaw ants feed on insects such as crickets. SOCIAL BEHAVIOR These trap-jaw ants live in small colonies of between five and forty workers. FUN FACT Some trap-jaw ants snap their jaws as a way to jump away from predators. One jaw snap can send an ant as high as 8.3 cm (3 in.) in the air. That would be like a 1.7 meter-tall (5.6 ft.) person leaping 13 m (43 ft.) high!

Snouted Harvester Termites

In the darkness of night on the African savannah, a colony of snouted harvester termites is active. Even though there are many thousands of termites in one large earthen mound, these insects can communicate. How? They use chemicals produced by their own bodies.

The termites may give off pheromones, which tell others what direction to travel down a trail when looking for food. In addition to communicating through chemical means, the snouted harvester termites also protect themselves from many predators this way. They secrete a mixture of chemicals. This mixture can cause serious damage to the kidneys, intestines, and nervous system of predators foolish enough to eat them. As a result, many animals leave these toxic termites alone. However, one of the snouted harvester termites' main predators is the aardwolf. Aardwolves can eat hundreds of thousands of termites in a single night but seem to be immune to the termites' toxin.

SCIENTIFIC NAME *Trinervitermes trinervoides* (harvester termite, snouted harvester termite) CLASS Insecta (insects) LENGTH Up to 6 cm (2 in.) for queens, less than 1 cm (0.4 in.) for other classes of these termites HABITAT Grasslands and savannah regions LOCATION These termites are found in southern Africa. NUTRITION Snouted harvester termites eat grasses. SOCIAL BEHAVIOR Snouted harvester termites live in colonies made up of many thousands of individuals. The members of these colonies have different roles to play. Some are soldiers whose job it is to defend the colony from predators. Others are workers. They dig tunnels, find water and food, and build and repair their nests (among other jobs). These termites are mostly nocturnal (active at night). FUN FACT The mounds of snouted harvester termites can reach a height of 100 cm (40 in.)!

Hunting in packs, these animals are swift and efficient at keeping themselves well fed.

African Wild Dog

It is morning on the plains of Zimbabwe. The sun is pretty low in the sky. A pack of African wild dogs is lounging about. Their patchy yellow, black, and red coats provide camouflage amidst the soil and short grass of their habitat. A few pups frolic and play fight while the adult members of the pack have other activities in mind. After a good night's rest, these dogs are ready for their dinner.

For a while, the pack lounges around. A mother dog grooms her pup. Suddenly, members of the pack perk up. Their large ears begin to swivel as they pick up the tiniest of sounds. African wild dogs have excellent senses of hearing. Something is coming their way.

Just moments later, several impala arrive at a watering hole in the distance. Breakfast!

With their thin, muscular bodies, the dogs in the pack are quickly on their feet. Their long legs are fast. One of the larger impalas is targeted. The pack tries to frighten and separate the herd. They chase the impala briefly and the prey quickly grows weary. The alpha-male dog grabs hold of its prey before it can get away. Other members of the pack also sink their teeth into the impala, tearing it apart. The scene is bloody, and rather gruesome. Some of the adult dogs back off a bit so that the pups can eat. They stand guard and wait patiently until it is their turn to eat.

In just minutes, the pack of African wild dogs has devoured the impala. Their powerful teeth easily crunch through even the bones of their doomed prey. Another successful hunt.

Fact File

SCIENTIFIC NAME *Lycaon pictus* (African wild dog, Cape hunting dog, painted hunting dog) CLASS Mammalia (mammals) HEIGHT 76.2 cm (30 in.) LENGTH 76.2–142.2 cm (30–56 in.) WEIGHT 17.9–35.8 kg (40–79 lb.) HABITAT From open plains like deserts and grasslands to sparse woodlands LOCATION These animals live south of the Sahara but their populations are largest in southern Africa and the southern sections of East Africa. NUTRITION African wild dogs are carnivores (meat-eaters). They eat everything from birds and rodents to antelopes and wildebeests. SOCIAL BEHAVIOR African wild dogs are social animals. They usually gather in packs of about 10 individuals, though sometimes packs can be as large as 40. The individuals in a pack are known to share food and also to help ill or weak members. Wild dog packs also hunt together, taking down larger prey like antelopes or wildebeests. FAMILY + OFFSPRING Females have litters of between two and twenty pups. The entire pack, not just the mother, cares for these pups. The dogs communicate by vocalizing and touching each other. After hunting, these dogs will regurgitate (throw up) meat for the pups to eat. AGE EXPECTATION (LIFE SPAN) Up to 11 years in the wild FUN FACT Unlike other dogs, these dogs only have four toes on their front feet. PHYSICAL DESCRIPTION These dogs have mottled, irregular coats with patches of black, red, brown, white, and yellow fur. Every African wild dog has a unique coat pattern. Their ears are round and large. CONSERVATION African wild dogs are endangered. Their population continues to decline because of habitat loss. These dogs are also threatened by conflict with people and by infectious disease. It is estimated that there are about 6,600 adult African wild dogs left in the world.

The Tale of the Elephant and the Wild Dog

Near an African village lived a huge, angry elephant. The villagers feared it. The village head promised a reward to anyone who destroyed the elephant. A wild dog said he could do this but that the villagers needed to clear a 32-kilometer-long (20 mi.) path first. When the path was finished, the wild dog challenged the elephant to a race. At every kilometer along the track, another wild dog hid in the grass, taking the place of the previous dog. The elephant and villagers never noticed this. At the race's end, the elephant dropped dead of exhaustion.

African Wild Dog

–

This pack of African wild dogs is on the prowl, searching for its next meal.

Incredible jumpers, elands also use many water-saving strategies to keep them alive in arid locations.

Eland

The eland is a resourceful creature. It has adapted to deal with living in the arid conditions found in many parts of Africa. When in the rainy season, elands sometimes live in huge groups of over 1,000 individuals. But what happens when water is scarce and the plants are bone-dry? Never fear, the savvy eland knows how to survive!
Imagine the waterholes are dried out. It is the heat of the day. The herbs and leaves that the eland prefers are far from moist. The eland plays a waiting game. Instead of wasting time and energy foraging for food during the daylight, it waits until nighttime. Why? Over the course of the night, the vegetation absorbs moisture from the air. So when the eland chows down on plants at night, its meal contains much more water content than it would have when the sun was high in the sky.
The eland has other tricks to conserve water, too. Instead of sweating to cool off, and losing a lot of its water, the eland has a neat trick. During the day its body temperature rises. This reduces the need for the eland to sweat. What happens after sunset? The eland is able to let some of its body heat radiate out into the night air, which is much cooler. Their bodies do not even waste much water in their dung, which is very dry, too!
Because of its water-conserving superpowers, the eland can go for fairly long periods without drinking water at all.

Fact File

SCIENTIFIC NAME *Taurotragus oryx* (common eland, eland) CLASS Mammalia (mammal) HEIGHT 1.8 m (6 ft.) at the shoulder LENGTH 2.4–3.45 m (8-11 ft.) for male head and body, 2.0–2.8 m (6.6–9.2 ft.) for female head and body, 50–90 cm (20–35 in.) for tail WEIGHT 590–680 kg (1,300–1,500 lb.) HABITAT Grasslands, acacia savannahs, alpine moorlands, miombo woodlands, subdesert areas LOCATION Elands largely live in eastern and southern Africa. NUTRITION Elands are herbivores (plant-eaters). They tend to eat leaves, fruits, bulbs, and roots. Eland calves nurse on their mother's milk for around three months. SOCIAL BEHAVIOR Younger elands may live in small groups. Female elands often live in groups with their young. Mature males usually form their own herds. Older male elands tend to be solitary. Females travel more widely than males. Elands are active at both day and night but often feed during the night. FAMILY + OFFSPRING The gestation period of elands is about 280 days. It is common for females with young calves to live together in what are called nursery groups. Female elands give birth to a single calf. They keep their new-borns hidden among the plants for the first two weeks. AGE EXPECTATION (LIFE SPAN) 15–20 years FUN FACT An eland can jump a 2.4 m high (8 ft.) fence from a standstill! PHYSICAL DESCRIPTION Elands are antelopes but many think they resemble cows. They change color as they get older. Normally elands are tan, tawny, or fawn-colored, but they become grayish and finally almost black as they age. Their horns are tightly spiraled. Males have a tuft of black hair that grows from the fold of skin hanging from their neck. Its mouth and muzzle are somewhat small and pointed. Their ears are also small and narrow. Elands have long tails with a tuft of black hair at the end. CONSERVATION The population of elands is declining. People prize them for their meat, milk, and hides. Elands are popular targets for hunters. As populations in Africa grow, people encroach on the habitats of elands. Sometimes their food sources and living spaces are destroyed in the process.

Southern Africa's San People and the Eland

The eland is very special to the San people of southern Africa. This animal is a major food source for them. The eland is also an important religious symbol to the San. They feel the eland represents both environmental and spiritual well-being. After an eland is killed, a spiritual leader invites the animal's spirit to enter his body. The eland's supernatural power can be used to make rain and for healing.

Active during the day, these birds use some clever strategies to protect their eggs.

Greater
Honeyguide

It is a sunny day in Mozambique. Amidst the scrublands, a Yao man searches for honey. Suddenly, a grayish-brown bird with a pink bill appears on the scene. The bird flutters in front of the honey hunter. Then it tweets at the man. The bird is a greater honeyguide. It flies from one tree to the next, seeming to guide the man to bees' nests hidden inside hollow tree trunks. Could this bird actually be helping the man? Absolutely!

Greater honeyguides are famous for increasing people's rates of success in locating bees' nests. Humans often make a special call to attract the attention of the greater honeyguides. In some places, the call may be a whistle. In others, it might be a "brrr-hm" noise. When they hear the call, the birds often guide people to honey. What is in it for the birds, you wonder? After the people use their axes to get the honey from beneath the tree bark, they leave behind the wax—the favorite food of greater honeyguides. It is a win-win situation for human and bird alike. Scientists think the relationship between humans and greater honeyguides is likely thousands or perhaps even millions of years old.

SCIENTIFIC NAME *Indicator indicator* (greater honeyguide) **CLASS** Aves (birds) **LENGTH** Around 20 cm (8 in.) for body **WEIGHT** 48.9 g (1.7 oz.) for average male, 46.8 g (1.6 oz.) for average female **HABITAT** These birds prefer to live in large, open areas. They can be found in shrubland, savannah, orchard, or riverside habitats. **LOCATION** Greater honeyguides live throughout much of sub-Saharan Africa. **NUTRITION** These birds have an unusual, wax-based diet. They have special enzymes in their digestive system so they can break down this wax. Greater honeyguides also eat insect larvae and grubs (of hive-dwelling insects) as well as fruit on occasion. **SOCIAL BEHAVIOR** Greater honeyguides tend to be solitary creatures except briefly during mating season. These birds are diurnal (active during the day). **FAMILY + OFFSPRING** A female lays four to eight eggs in a breeding season. She lays one egg per nest—but none of these nests belong to her. Instead, the female greater honeyguide puts an egg into another bird's nest, then pierces the hosts' eggs so her chick will survive. Nasty! **AGE EXPECTATION (LIFE SPAN)** Up to 12 years in the wild **FUN FACT** In Zambia, greater honeyguides are attracted to the sound of chopping wood.

Southern Yellow-Billed Hornbill

In a dry woodland area of Kruger National Park, a pair of southern yellow-billed hornbills is on a mission. They are looking for holes in tree trunks. Why? They want to find a nesting site where the female can lay her eggs. Ideally, they want to find a place that gets heat from the morning sun and is out of the prevailing winds. Once they choose a suitable spot, the female hornbill lines the base of the hole with pieces of bark or dry leaves. Then she does something that might seem strange. She closes up the entrance hole to her nest—with her own poop! She only leaves a small slit open so that her mate can bring food to her while she lays on her eggs. The female hornbill stays inside her sealed-up nest until her oldest chick is 3–4 weeks old. Then the chicks seal up the nest again and are fed through the slit by both parents. They stay there until they are old enough to fledge.

SCIENTIFIC NAME *Tockus leucomelas* (southern yellow-billed hornbill) CLASS Aves (birds) LENGTH 40 cm (16 in.) WEIGHT 153–242 g (5–9 oz.) for male, 138–211 g (5–7 oz.) for female HABITAT They live in open savannah and woodland areas. LOCATION Southern Africa NUTRITION Southern yellow-billed hornbills are omnivores. They mostly forage on the ground, eating seeds, fallen fruit, and small animals. They also eat insects. SOCIAL BEHAVIOR It is common for an adult male and an adult female to live together for the long term. These hornbills are diurnal (active during the day). FAMILY + OFFSPRING These birds make their nests in natural tree holes anywhere from 0.75 to 12 meters (2-39 ft.) above the ground. Females lay between two and six eggs (usually three or four), which they incubate for about 24 days. During this time, the male feeds the female through the entrance hole to the nest.

Laughing out loud, hyenas communicate many different messages to their peers.

Spotted Hyena

Out of the grasslands of southern Africa comes a funny noise. It sounds like a giggle or a laugh. But there are no people around who might be telling jokes. So who is making this silly sound? It is a clan of spotted hyenas.

Hyenas may be known for their giggles and laughs, but these mammals have quite a complex system of communication. These terrific hunters sometimes celebrate a successful hunt by making their laughing noise. The giggle lets other hyenas know that there is food to be shared. However, the giggle can also be a giveaway to other animals that a feast is not far off. Lions have even been known to engage in a game of tug-of-war with hyenas over fresh meat.

Sometimes a hyena's laugh is used when the animal is nervous and excited. Or when one hyena is being submissive to a more powerful or dominant hyena. But giggles are not the only sounds spotted hyenas make. Researchers have recorded more than 11 different sounds hyenas make. A "whoop" sound can be heard for kilometers and can be used to locate cubs, to bring the clan members together, or even to advertise territory. And the spotted hyenas can even tell which other individual made the whooping noise. These clever creatures greet each other with squeals and groans. Sometimes they growl and grunt at each other. Hear a strange sound off the beaten path from humans? It just might be a spotted hyena!

Fact File

SCIENTIFIC NAME *Crocuta crocuta* (spotted hyena) CLASS Mammalia (mammals) HEIGHT 77–81 cm (30–32 in.) at the shoulder LENGTH 1.2–1.8 m (4–6 ft.) WEIGHT 40–86 kg (88–190 lb.), 1 kg (2 lb.) at birth HABITAT Spotted hyenas live in most habitats in Africa. They can be found in savannahs, grasslands, woodlands, forest edges, semi-arid regions, and mountains as high as 3,900 m (12,800 ft.). LOCATION Spotted hyenas live in much of sub-Saharan Africa. NUTRITION Spotted hyenas are carnivores (meat-eaters). They eat animals as big as wildebeests and as small as insects or lizards. Hyena cubs nurse for one to two years. SOCIAL BEHAVIOR Spotted hyenas are social animals. They live in groups called clans. A clan may have as many as 80 members. Females lead the clans. FAMILY + OFFSPRING The gestation period for spotted hyenas is 98 to 111 days. Females often give birth to two cubs in a litter. Mothers keep their cubs in their own dens for about two to six weeks before they move to a den shared by other moms and cubs from the same clan. Male cubs stay with their mothers for about three years, while female cubs stay with their birth clan for life. AGE EXPECTATION (LIFE SPAN) 21 years FUN FACT Hyenas can eat one-third of their body weight in a single meal! CONSERVATION The population of spotted hyenas is healthy at this time. Sometimes humans kill hyenas when they prey on their livestock.

The Tale of the Hyena And The Hare

Hare and Hyena were bitter enemies. Every time they met, Hyena found that he wanted to eat Hare. But Hare knew Hyena was afraid of Lion. One day Hyena met Hare. Hyena asked where Hare had been and threatened to eat Hare if he did not tell. Hare said that Lion had told him to wait there so he could cook a hyena's liver for him. Hyena asked where Lion was. Hare pretended Lion was close by. Hare called out to Lion that he was following Hyena's footprints. Hyena heard this and ran into the bush. Hare laughed—and saved his own life.

Animal Allstars

African Animals Facts and Folklore

This book was conceived, edited and designed by Gestalten.

Told by Alicia Klepeis
Illustrated by Florian Bayer

Editorial Management by Maria-Elisabeth Niebius
Design and layout by Anna Berge
Typefaces: Nobel by Tobias Frere-Jones, Pocket Px
by Kemie Guaida, and South African by Måns Grebäck

Aardvark tale adapted from Awful Aardvark by Mwalimu
and Adrienne Kennaway.

Published by Little Gestalten, Berlin 2017
ISBN: 978-3-89955-782-4
The German edition is available under ISBN
978-3-89955-781-7

Printed by Offsetdruckerei Grammlich GmbH, Pliezhausen
Made in Germany

For more information, please visit little.gestalten.com.

Bibliographic information published by the Deutsche Nationalbibliothek:
The Deutsche Nationalbibliothek lists this publication in the Deutsche Nationalbibliografie; detailed bibliographic data are available online at http://dnb.d-nb.de.

This book was printed on paper certified according to the standards of the FSC®.